PARISH OF THE PHYSIC MOON

BOOKS BY DON DOMANSKI

The Cape Breton Book of the Dead (1975)
Heaven (1978)
War in an Empty House (1982)
Hammerstroke (1986)
Wolf-Ladder (1991)
Stations of the Left Hand (1994)

PARISH OF THE PHYSIC MOON

Don Domanski

Copyright © 1998 by Don Domanski

All rights reserved. The use of any part of this publication reproduced, transmitted in any form or by any means, electronic, mechanical, photocopying, recording, or otherwise, or stored in a retrieval system without the prior written consent of the publisher – or, in case of photocopying or other reprographic copying, a licence from the Canadian Copyright Licensing Agency – is an infringement of the copyright law.

Canadian Cataloguing in Publication Data

Domanski, Don, 1950-
    Parish of the physic moon

Poems.
ISBN 0-7710-2874-1

I. Title.

PS8557.O43P37 1998   C811'.54   C98-930179-6
PR9199.3.D65P37 1998

Typeset in Minion by M&S, Toronto
Printed and bound in Canada

We acknowledge the financial support of the Government of Canada through the Book Publishing Industry Development Program for our publishing activities. We further acknowledge the support of the Canada Council for the Arts and the Ontario Arts Council for our publishing program.

McClelland & Stewart
The Canadian Publishers
481 University Avenue
Toronto, Ontario
M5G 2E9

1 2 3 4 5   02 01 00 99 98

For Mary

*The seat of the soul is where the inner world
and the outer world meet. Where they overlap, it's
in every point of the overlap.*

— Novalis

*Invisible, visible, the world
does not work without both.*

— Rumi

CONTENTS

I SLEEP'S OVA

Writing / 3
Shadows / 4
Wings Black as Feathers Are Allowed / 5
Bay of Fundy / 7
Rain / 8
Every Night the Earth Is Drowned / 9
The Purest Myth of the Secret Country / 11
Pictograph / 12
Sleep's Ova / 13
Curtains / 15
Genius Loci / 16
Naos / 18
Table and Chairs / 19
The Card Players / 20
House / 22
The Passageway / 24
Death's Insomnia / 26
The Unknown / 27
Parish of the Physic Moon / 29

II WHAT THE BESTIARY SAID

What the Bestiary Said / 35
Dragonfly / 36

Owl / 37
The Blue Whale / 38
Mind of the Jellyfish / 40
Crow / 41
The Fox After Death / 43
Melencolia / 44
Osprey and Salmon / 45
Dead Fish on the Good Voyage / 46
Tonic's Dark Shoulder / 47
The Poem in the Hive / 48
Notre-Dame de Paris / 49
A Grieving Man / 50
Sentient Beings / 51
Ur-fish and Fingerlings / 53
Lusus Naturae / 54
Lynx / 55
Good Bruin in the Heart / 56
    1 Spring / 56
    2 High Bear in the Body / 56
    3 Foreland of Anatomy / 57

III THE SAYINGS OF DARK SPACE UPON THE BODY

Small Kingdoms / 61
Cloudbursts in a Lower World / 63
The Planet Asleep on Your Heart / 64
Taking the Train to Fredericton / 66
Miners / 67
Beefwood / 68
At the Height of Names / 70
The Invention of Palmistry / 71
Household Gods / 72
Locks and Keys / 73
In the Field of Orison / 74

The Leaf Opera / 76
Walking Away / 77
From Le Havre to Cork / 79
The Particulars of Pointed Things / 81
The Grass Widow / 82
The Sayings of Dark Space Upon the Body / 84
Arrows / 86

IV CHILD OF THE EARTH

Twelve Corners of the Earth / 91
    January / 91
    February / 92
    March / 93
    April / 94
    May / 95
    June / 96
    July / 97
    August / 98
    September / 99
    October / 100
    November / 101
    December / 102
Genesis / 103
Banns / 104
Child of the Earth / 105

Note on the Text / 108

I
SLEEP'S OVA

WRITING

a background of clouds
on my computer screen

at my feet the heavy tome of a cat
exhausted from reading
his covers closed for the night

on the roof insects
moving across gravel and tar paper
each of their bodies a caravan
almost lost   almost finding its way

above them bats fly through their own Cinemascope

silence like grass at sea level
feeling one damp breath after another
a coolness coming in from other realms

in vacant office towers across town
elevators are stables where horses and hay
are lowered slowly to the Underworld

cables surrounded by a pause in this poem
allow for their descent.

SHADOWS

on my way home I notice my shadow
carries the shadow of a bundle
which I don't have in my hands
a bundle the size of a baby
wrapped tightly in paper

perhaps it isn't a baby
but a cat from the other side of things
or a bell for a church deep in the earth
where stones have saints carved out of flesh
or it's simply groceries
provisions for a long night under my bed

the traffic passes by slowly
wheels in the heat smell of the roots of things
weeds   dead bodies   damp rocks
all doorways to the Underworld

my shadow makes the sign which says we should hurry
the bundle moves   impatient with this world

the sun is unbearable
the shadows of rain fall everywhere.

WINGS BLACK AS FEATHERS ARE ALLOWED

the radio misspelled everything
the room was tired
reaching in the dark for its chair

someone lay on the mattress
with a young woman
he was a stranger
complete with fallen angels
tattooed along both arms
angels that continued their fall
into her body

the young woman had this feeling
say it was feathers moving beneath her skin
like combs being slowly drawn through roses

say it was the body appeased
and the next shape of reason

the shape of flight cupped against the moment
say it was wings black as feathers are allowed
oncoming against the heart

that would be blessedness and hands
bound to desire
that would be enough to be human
to be lover
the life that reappears
at the end of each sentence
a life followed by clouds
out of which you can cry

it would be enough then to cry out
to be the animal built of dust
mended by images of dust
to feel combs being drawn through roses
to hold your flesh to the earth.

BAY OF FUNDY

for Ray

silence in the middle of the day
the sea repairing the heartbeat of a stone
among stones at my feet

this sun succeeding where all other suns have failed
to warm the dead in their chapter houses
their meeting places that weigh down the tips of the grass

I come here to feel the circumstance in the waves
the voice in the water drop that ends before it begins
to be still with that ending   that unreasoning

I come here so this place will ask things of me
ask me to be mute as the miracle inside the stone
those heartbeats like silver rummaging about in bronze
just that shining of sound   a chime and a darkness
a chime and a darkness and the heat of outer stars

I come to find the desire to believe in the moment
that was never time or time's vacuum
not the good ghost building the world or the death of ghosts
but tides borne up by the cerulean rise
of physiques within physiques
blue augmenting blue   ever-blue on ever-blue
lapis-life with nothing to be gained or granted
nothing lost and the love of unknowing on every side.

RAIN

the rain makes its way through rush-hour traffic
but it's not furious or tired
it has only these little efforts at being anywhere
at any particular time

little efforts like the smallest teeth
grinding against the largest door
and on the other side of that door
there are endless halls and rooms
containing the last five thousand millennia
containing no effort at all.

EVERY NIGHT THE EARTH IS DROWNED

beneath the ocean the land goes to sleep
the grain lies down   telephones disengage
powerful people weep into their fists
paintings slide from their frames

by midnight sharks swim by like heavy trucks
trucks carrying something black and miserable
bales of old phonograph records
78s of a lost voice rising out of the depths

by 2:00 a.m. turtles remove their shells
and are just like us only better at praying
making their gods out of storms and salt

people have so much work under the sea
the living ones must plot or dream
the dead ones must reach for pen and paper
which they never manage to touch

I do my best work at night
holding my pen tightly while I can
I write starfish on a page   I write shad
mullet   cod   I write flounder
I write because I can't swim
like my enemies can swim
their fins large as buildings
leaning into their own shadows

their egg-white teeth
their weeping lips

their tails moving rapidly from side to side
like nations measuring the darkness
like all the empires of the world.

THE PUREST MYTH OF THE SECRET COUNTRY

a bird stitched into the tablecloth flies below the supper dishes
long days are under the white plates now empty of food
the bird is flying over a country where the trees feign death
so as not to be seen
their salvation is that many have lived in that place
without knowing it
all of those rising from their chairs
had lives there once between the particles
cloistered beyond sight they knelt in the tranquillity
of calling out to each other
they had the faith of children then
they had a world of things to do.

PICTOGRAPH

1

I stand in an alley where all the stones lie
like broken wrists in the earth

a morning in September and this space between buildings
like the far end of a hospital ward
where faces gather in corners
before departing from the world

here an entity of formless duration inspirits
the place with sorrows that push against light
weeping being the oldest hymn   most ancient song
it stands and breathes among the apparitions you never see
legions of lost and possible shapes   the crowd half-spoken
scrivened on air   plainly visible to flesh but not mind
or eye secure in its watery resemblance to rain on good sleep.

2

there should be pictographs along these walls
as there are sometimes at the bottom of deep canyons
ones of spirits dancing
holding onto their green tongues with both red feet

this is a dry riverbed where a presence touches you
with the pastiche of considerable nothings
a presence like someone holding a ton of wilted flowers
an inch above your head and you sense that weight
and a voice is speaking and unspeaking in turns
saying and crackling and wishing to be near.

SLEEP'S OVA

the city is empty enough for offices
to fill with afterlives   which means
snow is falling on the streets
which means a dog is somewhere
which means the heart and liver are wet
with darker ages than the surgeons have ever known

I came to the city from the grasshopper's wing
from stones struck hard against a beach
from roots and frogs and my mother's hair

I was born because millions of years ago communities
grew out of ponds   because ponds need a way to say goodbye
because I'm always saying goodbye   and so are you

we grew up side by side
eye to eye through the rigging of tadpoles
out of sluggish heaven   out of sleep's ova
like flowers growing from the camera's hopeless light
that next photograph taken on the green

the snow comes because of desire
because it has to have its place beside the dust
because someone is changing horses in 1829
because someone is arguing with his wife in 2078
and this is the storm's way of listening to them
this silence in the streets   this wind blowing
all the gleams   blowing the loose railings
that lead your hands down into death

what I carry through the storm
is what I carry through sleep
the shadows of crows across my shoulders
tongue and groove of age across my face
the small cusps of history in my shoes
misspelled memories all along my spine

I'm walking headlong through the weather
the snow is a coastline
beyond it a spooled and posthumous forest
nothing scary   just that sleight-of-hand motion
of being born and dying and being born
a forest like a bedroom at night
when someone opens the door a crack
but nobody comes in.

CURTAINS

this is the good you do while you sleep
the feet you move when you dream

here you come and the caribou follow you
safely through the car cemetery
you're just about to lead them into the tundra
when the alarm goes off

you rise immediately
go to your window   throw back the curtains
and it's all there again
men in their legs   birds in their wings
the motion of mountains behind fish
and you hear the caribou whisper
from somewhere inside the room
that this is the building of the ordinary day
that all this is the dark figure in the spider's web
waving to God across time.

GENIUS LOCI

(second week of a coma)

I'm seated by calm waters
thinking of your fate
a garter snake appears
with the melancholy of idle hands
folded beneath each scale

does it know you

caddis flies gliding
their larvae rocking in their toothy cribs
glasswort touches the madtom's passing face
you feel that touch and it burns too bright

what form are you now
that you are neither dead nor alive
not emptiness or space filled
not darkness or the cosmetics of light
burning in the flesh

are you flesh   or afterflesh
what form do you take

are you seraphic with clouds
beneath your tongue
or daemon fetched a thousand times
from the backs of mirrors

does the pike see you
or the killdeer crying like a child-bride
among the reeds

is your mind rain falling
on the memory of leaves
your mind a bare floor
like the dancer's heart
can you speak now to the water drop
with its busy life   its many appointments
can you hear what the hydra says

some say you're in your hospital bed
with tubes like trailing grasses
emerging green from your body

I know better and I know worse

sad man the presences are you
the outer arabesques   the inner weavings
of the intermittent day

some travellers return
voices say that to the ears along a room
but I say there's nothing to return to
nothing you have left

no coming or going

love tells the secret   love repeats it
to each breath
and in the telling that secret is kept.

NAOS

it's getting dark in the small wood above the ravine
where the dead car is everything silent

there's one last goldfinch in the pine tree
a star about to lead her away

when I was six I was told this ravine
was where every fear came from
bogeymen with horns in their elbows
shuttling between marsh and closet
with their tooth and clamp and unreasonable ways

devils with mouths as wide
as double anything you might think of
eyes pin-curled to tongues
tongues the shape of balconies
where smaller demons stood
the ones that entered your body
via anus or ear

now it all seems comforting and small
like God and His forgiveness and His overnight bag
hidden somewhere deep in the church

now the ravine is a temple   naos
one of many layers leading up through time
along with devils   God   bogeymen
goldfinches   dead cars   stars
and now the murmur of power
a new presence down there withdrawing the silence
and the listening   the little ears
shattered among the stones.

TABLE AND CHAIRS

this room is the temperature of a rabbit's body
these chairs are what remains after all the violins
have been carved out of the tree
this table has carried the earth's motion for seventy years
and never put it down anywhere

sometimes in early morning light I sit
and listen to birds stirring
their songs enter this small room
like fine bone china sliding across the table
planks worn dark with the long distances
that birds immediately lean upon when they wake.

THE CARD PLAYERS

it's exactly noon and the honeycomb
purrs in the tree
mothers and fathers fail the air
falling backwards onto human things
cats sleep like cats in Erebus
or cats overseas or cats on Mars
and the children are playing cards
while dogs watch
as essential spirits
of any game that has no rules or purpose

the sun is outwardly part of the scene
but people on the sun
pay no attention
Mr. and Mrs. Helios who drink cold drinks
and look the other way

but they're the wrong ones
to judge this moment
the weight of clubs and hearts
upon the ether

the way these card players bring an intelligence
back to the devastations of time
that the turning of those cards
changes everything forever

the dogs know this and are mesmerized
calm as dogs drawn on a page
where the afternoons are smeared
where children laugh

their colours spreading the way Jove
spreads chocolate and thunder outside the lines.

HOUSE

glass huddled in its frames   doors knocking on doors
everything afraid the phone might ring
a voice might speak from far away
like bees hurrying through human words

she lived there as a child
tonight the house thinks of her footsteps on the stairs
remembers the margins of her desires
folding in immense pleats all around her
her heart placed just so   like gravity
holding flowers in a vase

tonight in a city hundreds of miles away
she's being told of a restaurant she has never met
where the cockroaches shine like mother-of-pearl
on the greasy faucets and walls
but the food . . .
the food is like cranes gliding in over marshlands at sunset

shimmering

she's lying in bed
the man beside her runs his hand down along her thigh
there's enough darkness in the room to fill a forest
the clock beside the bed glows white
the numbers are radiated teeth
from a mouth lying under the bed
another spirit no one understands

over her dresser there's a photo of the house
the ocean is also there in the upper-right-hand corner

the photo has faded just a bit
one gull and a few leaves on an oak tree have disappeared

as the man kisses her neck she thinks
of windows hung like portraits of great
invisibilities
the basement flickers in recall like a campsite at night
her parents with their mouths drawn tight   each day was
a blindfold
black birds flew in to cover their eyes before they rose
a childhood spent breathing under blank waters

the house is afraid of her memories
they grow each time as immense thickets
up through the bare floors
even the closets are afraid and they know little fear
the attic penetrated by starlings trembles
and the sink of dry leaves
the spook of a black phone that glides the air
would rather be alone with the surface of empty rooms
a phone which once listened to everything
knew all the emotions
all the human words.

THE PASSAGEWAY

the mind is emptiness or almost so
no more than the small space between
the horse's shoe and dry soil
no less than the gallop of a horse
across clefts of nothingness
under birches that lead to the river

the salmon in the river are almost so
still you hardly notice them holding open doors
decorated with venerable black gills
doors that breathe
that lead down into the earth

the passageway has no room for the mind
or the body with its needlepoints of sorrow
these must be left behind like clothes on a riverbank
along with the horse who knows the way so well

what's left of you must travel
like the child asleep in its mother's arms
but you're not sleeping
and you're no longer a child
you're a lamp through which fire passes
but you see no light   feel no heat
which means you're coming close
upon something that's motioning to you
down there in the darkness

it could be a swell of teeth
it could be a stranger or an enormous storm
or the deepest word that knows nothing of pity
or your strugglers with loss and desire

whatever it is you've been carrying it all your life
and must finally meet its gaze
eyelids that opened the moment you were born
when you rose up into the world

eyes that are creatures in themselves
that are slayer and slain
scream and whisper
all the shadows lying down.

DEATH'S INSOMNIA

all the dark departures from this world
are ears enough to hear the listening
of stones and grass
those wishes   those attentions paid to the air

Death listens to their hearing and it's like sleep almost
the almost-dream that comes with a voice
that saying of light's term upon distant ground
the speaking of time to come   life to come
tides in sand and painted veins
pulse of a heart peeling water from the shore

he has no sleep   this is as close as he can come
that things are born is sleep enough   dream enough
all the rest that's needed to begin his work again
that skill and stance   those gauzy nails
that brush their weave against the body
threads that will make all things slumber
fall forward in their blood
into their voices and never rise.

THE UNKNOWN

I imagine the oddest things
oyster beds that run like foxes
along the bottom of the sea
a momentary virgin who foretells the birth
of a sentimentalist out of a cloud
inscrutable hearts that ordain dogs
in Ireland while they sleep

yet I can hardly think of myself
or imagine who I am
I can never come forward   just think of it
the dust along a psalm knows more

do I have hands   legs
a twinning of touch and membrane
or am I all branches   treetops filling
with lightning and the X-rays of crows
a shoreline tethered to a moon
a rock   a turnstile beside the graves
of everyone who has been betrayed

white clothes are lying in the grass
they're alone   they might be mine
the pockets are full of split seconds
moments when you remember your name
when the mind shakes   spilling a drop of something
dark at your feet   an initial
the first clue that the day is bright
that you cast a shadow as long as Caesar
by merely picking up a stone

I cast no shadow   I'm a floor
where the footsteps of the miracles are heard
their waltz is like knives and scissors
dancing through the flesh
I know their appearance   their names
their shadows overflow   arrive and overflow.

PARISH OF THE PHYSIC MOON

for Julia

1

there were tenements of shadows
left behind in the grass
by rabbit and deer
poor men hid in them trying to stay warm
hunters without fires or homes to return to
dead men lost behind a leaf

there were fireballs set in motion
by any movement of the eye
pupae chanting
plaster falling from the moon
bees asleep like lovers
dissolving their edges round a sigh

grass held stars and the night
night without memory
without the little town
rooms composing light out of voices
outstretched candles made to flicker
like breath against chalk on a board
where the calculations were written
which no one believed
the mathematics of Euclid
moving endlessly round the sun.

2

it was difficult for her to bear the temper of birches
their emotional walks down to the river

hard to live with all those presences among the trees
snakes placing subspaces beneath every movement
each fox a spirit of dominions overgrown with existence
patterns implacable   rituals merciless
hawks in their banners   mice in their afterlives

and the sounds among the roots
were like a din of clouds in a tomb
rattle of arrows in a cathedral
sounds that foretold the coming of reality

roots where prayers drank up the water
a tight array of believers
a continuous gratitude   dark nunneries in the soil.

3

the sleeper was ill in her sleep
while all about her was the panacea
of time and white houses
the sanative cloud   physic moon
healthful stars
burning new worlds out of old
which is called time passing
which is time light years away
in the same room

the sleeper was expected
a luminous malady to fill the spaces
the invisibilities that made the sign of the miracle
which was the sleeper in her bed
heartsick   exhausted
a woman who made the dark crossing
and the world that followed her
was a divine world
where the wind blew blood into the heart
night directly into the mind

she with the grief of palms folded
over a will adorned with transmutations
of courage wounded   inhaled along a vein
with the grief of lines shaken loose
from the outline of blood on the floor

she called out to the moonlight for a remedy
to the trees weighted down with occupations
most unfathomable and sure
for the umber town to rise into those trees
to meet the invisible which would be old medicine
whisperings and activity
the healing of small sounds in the flesh.

4

so the town in time's light held on to the branches
to the location of time's judgement
the place where each tree met a sonorous god
his song done and undone by what's true

oh tremble me there said the sleeper
among the rush of ghosts under the bark
who raid the world that I conceived

but the sleeper only heard herself speaking
without knowing those words were the antidote
counterpoison that would phantom a cure
but the sleeper heard nothing but herself speaking
in the little town pressed between the pages
of a book not yet written   pages not yet numbered
her voice wrote the sentences on paper yet to be made
author of bindings and breath falling
and a calling across eyes closed

oh tremble me there said the breath drifting
to hidden places   to wounds secret
and abreast like crowds waiting

in rows as crowds in Pangaea
might have waited for what was missing
the turning of a page   the white beneath the words
words that didn't exist except as scales along the back
fear along the pubis and hearts like church bells underwater
tolling a sleep upon the sleep already there.

II

WHAT THE BESTIARY SAID

WHAT THE BESTIARY SAID

after many sorrows and thoughts broken
body pains and blows to the heart
after living in poorer lands
with human company in every mirror
I remembered what the bestiary said
and allowed the deer of the slender sadness
to take my voice and my hearing
the wolf of the impenetrable eyes
to remove my flesh and bone
the salmon to take my spirit
and I lay on lichens worn clean
by whispers close to the ground
so that I was the nothingness there
with only the beetle's breath to carry me till morning.

DRAGONFLY

my wings barely reach into the outer world

I dart through the swarm entangled in Eros
picking hearts like straws out of their bodies
picking blank eyes off such grinning faces
tearing out the sexual interiors
hinged all along their backs

I eat because the inner world
wants some longing at the crossroads
some hunger in the wingspan

three millimetres above the pond
is where you meet the gods coming through
clad in threads   in millions of deafening scratches

I bow down before them   I'm so many jagged points
along a second of ecstasy
I'm so many dark crowds visible unto death.

OWL

the timberline is all driftwood
floating in from the millennium
the bogs search for pleasures
that only a mother could provide

I'm a few feathers and a clock face
the presence of clasped hands in the tree
of a fist succeeding in the democratic air

each of my wings is a district that knows of no other
I'm carried along by the suspension of disbelief
holy   holy   holy
it's silent and dark and the shadows are rising
the spirits of bears lift the trees
mice follow me into the air.

THE BLUE WHALE

for Barry and Karen

I sat in the forest a long time
before I was born
with the dead and their skinny fires
with ants who lowed like cattle
in ravenous sleep

call me possible   I was that
and a little steepness in the void
a swelling of outgrowths
a clotting of leaves

I sat and the wind made
the tops of the trees sound like a tavern
where a stranger bought drinks for everyone
and paid with gold

I stood and the wind brought my footprints
and I walked in them beneath the boughs
walked in the ingredients   in mouthfuls of segments
in all the tasty accidents of the leaf mould

few paths lead to oblivion   I found none
and so was born to the contradictions
of my mother's body
to that great slab of rain and flesh
and so lost my legs
my restless arms

I flippered into
the first ocean that I saw
such confidence there
I took the stars down with me
and my wild mother
with her darkening hills

massive we were
so far away from moonlight
and our footsteps   disembodied
well   you could hear them still
encircling trees and roads
walking along fences
entering farmhouses

the footprints of oceans
left on pine floors
the sound of granite
falling on flowers

we ran our absent hands along blankets
we walked into walls
we were that full of joy.

MIND OF THE JELLYFISH

no one thinks of this Cambrian tent with its blue legs
red feet that dangle among the numberless places
blown forward by time
you could say its mind is china broken and mended
broken and mended every other minute
you could say its mind is as silent
as hospital buildings late at night
where the fingers of the sick beat
like ten hearts at their sides
and each beat is a brooding
upon oceans forgotten
waters where the Mystery
began to excite itself with names

you could say anything and all at once
it would be true and nothing
you could say anything
so I say its mind is a pair of folded hands
holding a glass ball which it never lets go
unless you mention it as I just have

the ball falls   glows from within   it's the colour of falling
inside it a single thought moves against the glass
shivers because it's alone.

CROW

when I appear the esplanade of angels
becomes an artifice   a dam of pig's feet
holding back the clouds

I'm the fingertips that move
the pieces across the board
when the board has been discarded
among graves and goslings
the hand in the window that starts to wave
hours before anyone appears

own me and I will stop the pouring down
the wet armies that fly out of trees
to pick the coins
from between your ribs while you sleep

pet me just along my back and wings
all my deaths lie like feathers there
all my ancestral futures are arranged for flight
and a smattering of torments to keep me warm

feed me with that hand
that glove of skin and divinations

in turn I'll give you
the thousand crows you'll feel fly past
each time you turn to satisfy a fear
I'll give you the blood-soaked bread
a place on the wires above the railway station
a view of the figure in the doorway
the man in the black hat

who snaps his eyes and beak
and flies away
who crinkles through so many foldings of the air.

THE FOX AFTER DEATH

there are silk climbs
and burlap climbs
places for me to go

as the spider goes
but with the sense of joy
a thousandfold

shine after shine
is the only way to describe death
bloodshine untranslatable
and flesh like clouds in the distance

having once been a fox
I flow like a river now
inside flinches of light
this must be the way
to the present
to an animal place
a dry field
that slowly pushes
its sticks into God.

MELENCOLIA

fine bronze heads and reunions in the grass
a frost so near and so a time
for an absence of goodbyes

for crickets an absence of goodbyes
is all they have   such divinations
and preachings and high births that granulate
beneath autumn winds

in a week they'll be old engravings   each a Dürer print
complete with those lines that twist themselves
finally into the shapes of saints and sinners
threadbare cloaks with gothic faces barely attached

their eggs lie buried in the dark soil all winter
each one looking like the mountain pass
where the expedition was lost
the abandoned wasteland where the small fire
was braided and lit   the flames that always consider
silence the first escape   the body's birth.

OSPREY AND SALMON

wings extended   gliding

dark pulse suffering fields of light

inside it all the mirrors fall silent
no images are cast   no sun or clouds
no threshold opened or closed

morphology of pure form
pinions that shudder against oblivion

it watches cream-coloured eyes at the water's edge
eminence of wadded feet along the shore
grottoes in a shell   mangers in a death
drifting on foam   bodies uncreated
among columns of reeds

the world arrives just as it descends
centuries return to their positions
along empty space

it dives towards the water
a fall withdrawn into eyesight

the salmon is astonished to find
that its fins will concede to the spirit of other things
that its gill openings hold all the names of God
deity and being
the full white solitude of death.

DEAD FISH ON THE GOOD VOYAGE

in the fishmarket at night
lying side by side on beds of salt
the fish lit up the building
their eyes full of candles
older than paradise

they lay there with
one last great space to swim across
the bald of interstice
noose-hole of the water drop
netherworlds placed at intervals

deeper and deeper they travelled
heaven's vertigo through all the oceans
that rose up to meet them on the other side
all the oceans that fell into that vacancy

oceans fell into that vacancy
into the little strokes   beating of fins
against all the chemistries
that make up what is passing right now
for time and flesh   what I am dying into
the knowledge of sequences   of death
lived and divided by ecstasies
the rapture that the water will wash away.

TONIC'S DARK SHOULDER

at daybreak the crows pour like medicine out of the trees
a tonic's black shoulder
nudging all those who know they'll leave no trace behind
which is everyone who is weak   which is everyone

scatter the weakness then on wings through brickyards
steelworks   bedsteads
human souls bellied with undertakings as mad as linen
holding back tears

the chaff of haunts between feathers
is so close to human things
human circuits that go round the boatslip
and garbage dump endlessly

they roost in more than branches
in the room's deepest corner their feathers stubble
such passageways that nature allows between worlds

they are the dark holding which takes us home to wake
atoms of a single hand spread across the earth
fingers picking up such shadows that we drop
behind us like slips of felt   margins of assent

a shawled breath that has been breathed upon by quotations
from the forest   small hours around the base of pines
that fly up   dry wings against the backs of our legs
as they run to crossroads to be early risers
running to bed to wake   to begin the unlearned day
again and again.

THE POEM IN THE HIVE

sound of a typewriter in the beehive at night
the queen writes her poem by the glow of a small shadow
which is a lamp ablaze in all other worlds but this

her sisters hold the heaviness of the page
which is sleep cleansed of absolutes
well stuffed with snowy wax and wounds that pass for clouds

the queen writes to a spirit that can only be calculated
by sums falling into infinity
like sovereigns falling among the most common men
among dirt and sticks and hunger under everything

her thoughts are drops of blood
rouged honey sweet with necessity
an intangible wisdom
the health of what you can't see in the dark
what's constellated beyond the eye   the bull in the hive
the generation in the poem   the bee in the moon

she writes and is queen and has the name of a girl
her name comes forth like a sea floor under a drowning
when it is heard among flowers or a blending of tempests
that name which says nothing survives the poem in the hive
not a dowager on six crutches or a crying winter
not an arrow in the flesh or a foothold in the world

every royal line leads to disinheritance
the moment rests on this.

NOTRE-DAME DE PARIS

there's no other creature like it
no beast covered in fists
no massive skull so full of unshakeable quakes
no Jesus as dark as this Jesus
nailed by its limbs to the earth

standing inside you hear a choir of shells
more than one ocean misunderstanding the earth
the elements risking everything by keeping still
the crashing waves hidden in icons
in candles   in those kneeling figures
who hold the ebbing waters in their hands

who hold themselves gently   those great animal hearts.

A GRIEVING MAN

the priest's house is made of feathers   black feathers
with dry blood down the shafts

outside grasshoppers lie still in the weeds
and on the stone steps a grieving man waits
blue lice in his hair
like a horse's mane blue with starlight

he carries messages from Death
both elbows have small wings like hummingbirds
his teeth are flesh   his hands bone
he's in league with all that's holy

the grasshoppers all hold wafers in their mouths
they're old churches without congregations
and are ready at any moment to leap clear of the earth.

SENTIENT BEINGS

in the abattoir after closing hours
when the walls and floors
smell sweet as taverns
warm as bedrooms where children sleep
when the fifty meat cleavers and the two hundred knives
hang from wooden pegs shining
like ice skates
and bloodied aprons are no longer flags
hung at all the entryways of death
you hear a whisper distant and alone
no crying any longer   no sobbing
no piercing screams obstructing the ceiling fans
just this rustling of a tongue
between two dry leaves in a corner somewhere
a feather between two stones

and the whisper is like a salamander descending
an immense staircase on such small legs
that the fatigue almost makes it stop

the whisper is our longing
for the inner eyes of the predator
teeth of the insectivore
a herbivore's composure
all the marine animals we wish we were
birds that simply fly away
those invertebrates that mate with a flame
inside their deepest selves
those larvae that need and know of nothing
but the earth's hold on duration

it asks "Where is the total weight
of being alive?"

it asks "Where are all the dark paths that lead
our lives astray?"

UR-FISH AND FINGERLINGS

one breath across a mirror and the day appears
along the glass   a dirt road released from the earth
the sun warming the depths of the entozoon
a palm reader just waking with both palms between her legs

the sun intended the palm reader and the grass
and the fingerlings in the brook who merge at night
with the Ur-fish of incoming fables

sometimes when I can't sleep I think of the Ur-fish
and the fingerlings out there in the darkness
in the narrow brook that runs cold even in high summer
near the dirt road and the palm reader's house

I wonder what they're thinking and even if it's nothing
I try to imagine the sheer weight of that against
the fact that I can't sleep
there's a knowledge there
gathered through time that frightens me
a depth that trembles insomnia to its bones

on two occasions I made love to the palm reader
both times she was the Ur-fish and I the fingerling
of the bulging eyes and open mouth
each time I gave up thinking afterwards and fell to sleep
while the cold waters carried us along
slowly like breath across glass
the little mist from between the lips that starts the day.

LUSUS NATURAE

for Tara

a rubbing of the moon appears above the lake
among trees beside those waters a creature is born
a tide moving outward among the trunks
trembling like oil sheeted with blood
no mother to nurse it   no father to protect it
it's the Divine coming into being again
Dark Slayer on the surface of darkness

it yawns with a wide slope of energy down into nothingness
its teeth weigh as much as fists
its mind is a heart beating in black strokes
escorting only one thought through the damp brush
while grinding its ribs against death in elementary circles
circles that are lenses above each hidden life

when it arrives in the city it'll be seen as falling leaves
as the shadow that occupies the empty coffee tin
clouds returning with the scent of the sea along their edges
small acts of fear will carry it to our bodies
where it will feel like rain upon us
the wind blowing   insects landing in our hair
we will call it a quiet anxiety   a mood
a memory we forgot we had

deep inside we'll know better
feel it shake its skin tight to the bone and throw back its head
from treetop to treetop we'll hear its voice move the branches
and know we are lost   finally beautiful
swallowed by the world.

LYNX

I have come to the Land of Forms
because there are others like me
we come to imagine ourselves

because snow is half the body
belief half the mind

our feet are soft dark ears
faithful hearing of faithful loss
we listen with the roots of trees
the rabbits ripen   ripen and fall to earth
we approach making them red with predestined wounds
the quiet sequences   the great turbulence
among the sounds that wish to be.

GOOD BRUIN IN THE HEART

1 SPRING

the earth is home from winter   from snow and ice
speaking together   leaning on the same sticks

the tide rolls against its own thoughts
echoes of driftwood against stone
the ocean's treetops swaying against the land

land which is now birth and straw
and standing descriptions of fallen things
once fallen in tragic weather to lie between
the thistle's bones   now returned to desire.

2 HIGH BEAR IN THE BODY

you use two dreams when you walk here
your belief and your grief to traverse wet ground
rain-soaked grass occupying a lifespan between the trees
birches shifting their weight from root to root
the movement of gathering light among black fish
Eocene waters now dried to time's soil

in these woods the bear inside the chest grows large
high bear in the body castling soul for flesh
essential snout so near to what the mind would like to be
toothed and ripest mouth against skin warmed
by the motion of organs repeating all the names of spirits
that existed once as every human need.

3 FORELAND OF ANATOMY

that deep bear   good bruin in the heart   fears for you
binds you to what you know is true or what you hope is true
takes the moment and makes it sublime   as the green darner
is sublime   a moment's description of what the mind seeks

crevices you against all appearances   hides you
from the pain of dogs and children in the yards at night
spoondrift of traffic   hospitals where doctors draw
their own breath up through dark incisions
the full moon pulling lightly on their surgical gowns
businesses that can't fall asleep until this age dies
maelstrom of all the screens   endless flood of tired speech

hides you between the sutures of grass   beneath the light
beneath the weight gone out of the burden
where the divine is thorn   reed   the salamander's sun
burning in its orbit under leaves
and planetary voices in the hills
where the divine is the birch tree and beneath the birch tree
and above is what heaven makes of its own magnificence
a millimetre of flame to every mile of ocean
cloud and star   the comet that burns outward from the eye
that deep bear   good bruin in the heart
braces you with workings of earth   foreland of anatomy
dandles the blood   speech that comes with the blood
bleedings of air   the flecks along the path.

III

THE SAYINGS OF DARK SPACE UPON THE BODY

SMALL KINGDOMS

1

dogs roam the streets of this small town
when everyone is packed in sleep
beside Diogenes and Novalis

from their beds the sleepers
nuzzle the low hills without knowing
lie beside their mother on damp ground
nursing from two shadows
sentience and forethought
dark breasts that keep them in the world

experiences gutter from their wet lips
not their own memories but all the fear
the dead had while still alive
fear of falling deeply into
the scent of mown wheat
into soft wings
sparrows that flew
above every treasure   every jewel
flew across wisdom
without longing for wisdom.

2

I agreed to love you most at this hour
when I sit apart from the sleepers in their blankets
and the dead in their lockets
when a stray shadow wanders through the backyards

the neighbour's old cat worn down by moonlight
whose legs only whisper to the earth
whose shoulders hold up the small kingdoms
of eternity and desire

I agreed to love you most at this hour
when the Mouse Galaxies rise above the horizon
Little Ghost Nebula
when a spider hangs from multitudes
celebrating an individual's place upon its ropes
a spirit crawling past flesh like wax
dripping to the floor

I agreed because at this hour I feel less myself
see less with a human eye and so take up my life again
as if it were whole
as if I could satisfy a moment of being
long for the foldings of forms not myself
as if there were forms not myself
love accomplished   existence contained
as if it were all foregone in dogs barking
cats leaping   stars burning down
to spiders and wax
as if my shoulders could hold up
the present moment that scuffs the grass dark
grass that is counterpart to secrets held
one secret that banks the fires above our heads
flames scratched by the essential moment of grief across light
the small kingdoms of eternity and desire.

CLOUDBURSTS IN A LOWER WORLD

rain falling on the garden frontiers
thunder rolling out of decimal points
far above the city
everyone running for cover

standing in my doorway
I thought of prenatal darkness
full of rain and the swelling of cellars out of flesh

I thought of what merges with rain
the grey time inside us
all the ministries of the unseen
saturated with the moment
our being adrift on cloudbursts
patient with ourselves for once

a blue rain fell in the yards
and that falling was a long life
an unknown heart resting in the air
so that afterwards we would hear
its beating when we reached for meaning
for a body or a hand

afterwards each blade of grass
gleamed like a fishing lure
stones seemed to have moved
closer to each another
which was only me searching
which was longing and nothing else
the homelessness of all the lower worlds.

THE PLANET ASLEEP ON YOUR HEART

I love you   so imagine you
on this rough night
with the wind blowing open
the houses of sparrows
houses that always please the earth twice
once in their building
once in their falling into the grass

I imagine you naked   hidden between
rain and your own flesh   breasts
that are rooms where the heron's feathers collect
when they've loosened their hold on the world
small rooms where silhouettes undress
after living so long in the snail's shell
in the hawkweed   in whitecaps
that turn their breath into shorelines
into pastures where the sounds of oarlocks
are heard in the cattles' hooves

your nakedness covers these hours
like an eyelid slipping over
a house and a road and a star
so that an inner light wreathes the self
the hand held out to the darkness

I know your body wishes to be strong
so it can dream of weakness
long for the empty space that can't be lifted
the sex of breaking out of time for an instant only
the planet asleep on your heart

I know that between your legs old journeys rustle
against the gathering fabric while you sleep
there the sparrow's house is built
the sparrow's house falls away
there the edge of the forest reaches first light
the dead pass the living and the day is made.

TAKING THE TRAIN TO FREDERICTON

we're moving through dark hills
forest on either side of us
the woman with the Harlequin romance
is sound asleep using her thigh as a bookmark
the old man next to me makes the noise
of a smaller train with each escaping breath

beneath us it feels like loose handshakes
coming together   coming apart
giant hands that otherwise would be
tearing trees out of the earth
or obeying a power greater
than the stealth of engineers

we lose our strength by just sitting here
tire of newspapers and conversations
nothing to watch out the windows
except a moon where they get the luminous clock face
the winding sheet   sand for the hourglass

but sometimes you see a square of light in the blackness
a couple seated at a kitchen table with a child between them
or a family gathered around a television screen
and it always feels like part of your life   part of your past
for a split second you feel excitement   a reaching back
then the forest reappears and you can't see once again
having gone too far back in time
where time is untranslatable

cells divide in shallow pools
one small blindfold growing out of another.

MINERS

coal miners come home to their beds
come to the surface of the earth just to lie down

large bodies hang loosely in sleep
like the sleeves of a T'ang scholar
bowing to his lord   grateful for even a reproach
to hear his master's flutist clear his throat before playing

it's been raining just a little but all afternoon
fences appear like musicians behind dark music.

BEEFWOOD (Halifax Harbour)

for Bert and Olga

I walk along the waterfront
small hours fall slowly upon the waves
slow as porcelain falls to the lips
its white sides held by fingers
absorbed with intent

the wharf carries great loads
of light in its timber
sun of forests   of hawks
dropping into the stems of fleabane
carrying off mice with feet broken
by sorrow   by the rolling of mist
through the heart

a containership sways in the dark
sailors move beneath its deck
shifting their weight around a word
without saying a word
on wide feet the language heaves
but never breaks through at this hour

the containers are filled with the wood
of the Australian pine
a tree that yields heavy red lumber
called beefwood
the word beefwood is a longing for land
a wild hill and a host of wings gliding

beefwood is the whale's memory of land
before the sea came courting the grass
with its needle-shaped babies and dragon's mane

beefwood is the dusty place behind the eye
where the ghost rages   a risen presence
rutted with particles of temptations
where temptations no longer exist

beefwood is a scriptural passage
now lost to black waters
good proverb thinned to prenatal tissue

I walk along the harbour thinking of trees and water
the wharf is a narrow ledge around the earth
below me I see the inner world   its red interior
the wood grain moving towards us on all sides
a fierce continuum   the reaches of certainty
a low place moving at the velocity of light.

AT THE HEIGHT OF NAMES

one evening in October
among the clatter of foundlings in the grass
pleating of crickets by the frost
he walked as men do upon the great space of the ground
and meditated on love as men do
doubly meditated with both sleeves of the mind
to call forth handless gestures that pick up fire
and place it at a human height
at the height of names so it burns
so the sheen is one of identity
the face is one you know

he walked down streets lined with elms   maples
the tinge and escape of darkness among their forms
symmetrical as numberless throats risen
all at once beyond sound   he moved beyond sound

he walked which was desire longing for motion
for thoughts that answer footsteps
because longing was like that
and like the contents of a feather   its many rooms
filled with the vatic hues of the horizon
so it could glide across the land enveloped in time
which was his desire   love's desire to be cometary
to fly past birds of good family and endure.

THE INVENTION OF PALMISTRY

the owl sleeps   giving off sunlight
far below on the forest floor
red ants build
one black needle for the length
of white thread they found in the road
there are no tailors among their kind
no garment makers
their master is the farmer's daughter
the grunting girl
the suffering one
she will sew for them
they will take her below
this voice of summer
this youthful hope
she'll backstitch and hemstitch
and seam the deepest worlds
she'll meet Death in their tunnels
and sew for his hands a line of destiny
a line of fate and a line of heart
and along his eyes the lines of laughter
but not the line of life which would anger him

she'll rule there as queen
and fill slowly with honey
and Death will pass them by
Death will read his fortune in the stitchings
of such moments that are his hands
and pass them by.

HOUSEHOLD GODS

it's the god in the table
in league with the god in the bookcase
that makes this room seem so small and empty

outside the city drifts among newspapers
rain falls in songs   in partnerships
moon is up   harm's way half-risen

this room is muffled by the god in the walls
who is forever wandering   recrossing his shadow
anxious to be the Lord of Hosts
redeemer of all space
his small hands are two men nervous
at any distance from one another
they avoid touching the same object
this room where I sit turning the pages
of a book without reading

while above me the god in the ceiling hears
all the movements of heaven
suns gnawing on driftwood
nebulas swallowing infinite numbers
galaxies preparing light on a black surface
cutting of worlds and stars
processing ice and fire

pitch of a spoon   the stirring of broth

eternity crossing the palate

kitchen sounds.

LOCKS AND KEYS

the dead man lies in a field beside a river
weeds study the sky   stars crackle in the crisp air
a bear comes and lays its head on his chest
an angel comes to count his eyelashes one last time
an otter comes to choose from the man's memories
a recollection that suits it best   one without thirst or hunger
something sweet to take back to its dark waters

the dead man has a key in his pocket
the lock is two hundred miles away waiting for his return
from deep inside there's a slight whispering
the turning of a key that isn't there
tongue in the mouth that mustn't speak up
not in this dreadful place   this world
where doors never open by their own accord

the dead man now sees that the passageway
to the next world is made of peace and axe blows
woven so tightly together it feels like flesh against the spirit
but any lock knows this prayer of travelling
any key could point you in the right direction
any doorway could tell you where the new day begins.

IN THE FIELD OF ORISON

1

wonders that will never cease   rain
growing old among the nettles
snails treasuring their single heartbeat
sinews in the weevil's jaw tightening
around a point in time
graves of deep oceans surfacing among the five senses
owls feathered past the mere shapes of a world
alders leaning into the womb's psalm   its deepest words

what is holy meets me in this field   divine presence
the toil of bogwater against jawbone
against the trench of the eye lost to death and death's weather
groundlings uncradled among outcrops
ore transfixed by outlying winds   by the curve of the earth
joined lips parting on blood
sacred haem   numinous dunghill   guttural clottings
of the heart   apparitional incisions
beading of grass through flesh
caries shedding their branchings of dissolve in unison

dimensions meet me along this derelict path   I'm blessed
by safeholds dotting gravity   workings of sanctuary
my body is lived in by two worlds
by surroundings I will never meet   I turn to them here.

2

tonight I come to pray for her   rush to her the harrier's wing
nod of the cricket's head   ply of the deer's rale
semitone of weeds running deep into the hills
all the hares a fox attends   I pray to her the chemistry
of stars   if not stars then tongues underleaf
hurry to her the ditch's breath   sweet decay of birth in water
speed her to words   stead of words
retrieved from grass   air   the driven loss
between hours spent with rain sagging so directly from clouds

I stand in this field and pray my life to her
which is only fitting   since I'm only this place barely changed
barely named   where I rose up I will fall   here
orifice grown perpetual   compaction of birth and death
upon each instant   upon the moment's panoply
I pray for her now   low simmer I feel   glints in the flesh
shadows fanning out of flesh   foreshadows come back to me
I pray her home in time   this field's sense of time
the present   the loam's measure   moment of everywhere.

THE LEAF OPERA

it's true the vetch perished   tare of the high hill
perished back to their dusty selves along the roadside
and that everything is unintelligible when
the heart struggles and this cold weather is its result

it's true I think of you during this opera of leaves
flying through these empty streets   dark houses
staged with dormant families   curled cats
and I feel the pitch of the wind as perfection
when I think of you   your absence
becomes more than a gesture but a longing
for your body's deepest breath   the words you spoke
your eyes shifting essences so that I thought of stars
Beta Orion   Regulus   burning with shapes not fire
burning colours at the back of the mind

the wind shakes the ribbons that hold the hours in place
the time it takes for time to pass   swoon of time
which tonight is the falling of leaves redescribed
by a consciousness created when any two fall together
the distance at which they fall   the nothingness between
the man walking between them thinking of you once again

loving you for having lifted the dust that turns the world
for having shaken the world so the dust fell upon his eyes
so he saw what form dust could take
braiding of earth and light
your body described in the leaf's missal   night's ledger

your deepest breath upon the trees.

WALKING AWAY

what does it mean to walk away from everything
reeds so still along the riverbank
like the eyes' motion held back against the heart
the water is a binding of one day to another
but never the day you live in at the moment

I walk and the hills are straining
in the stamens of asters held away from the wind
walking among spruce trees that fence in
a private light around each piece of dust
around each dandelion seed shaped like a casket
worn down by children inhaling sorrow
from inside its plush interior

wandering away from everything
passing the miles from hand to hand
the wings of sparrows hide in the cheekbones of deer
when my footsteps are heard in the brush

I want to go north to meet a dry leaf
a flake of snow
to witness a bear's hibernation
the energy that lives on in its paws
that gathers up the dark
from around antlers on the forest floor
the light from the labour of bees
passing directly through the sun

a bear in winter is like the Virgin after her son's death
it dreams of the heat of the good   blood of almsgivers
the medicine of walking for a month without stopping

then lying down upon brown twigs that held up the ancients
their robes stiff as bark   their hands hunting in their pockets
for stars and the father of stars   the slightest thing

I walk northward   cries of loons feed the pine needles a faith
curled tightly around rain and the shafts of feathers
the pine trees lean inward like sentries guarding things unborn
they know the nourishment of drifting
through secrecy after secrecy
their roots halfway down into bedrock
root hairs following the blonde caravans to Elysium
the dark processions to Tartarus
they know those paths and roads   the stones in the road
what it means to walk away from everything.

FROM LE HAVRE TO CORK

a settlement of light on the ocean surface
the past beaded throughout the water
like jewellery approaching skin
but never touching skin

I've been on this boat all night
and at last the moon has risen full
the only dry land the eyes can find
a plate of gravel   the big gaze above the sea
ashen and primal as gravity under tree roots
or the scaffolding that holds a breath in place
alongside the rapid movement of fear across skin

fathoms below the dead reach up
and touch each wave that approaches
to overlay them with allurements   a smoothing
of fingers against the bow   an exacting
of goodbyes that dissolve around us
like greetings from the oldest possible story

there are schemata floating through the air
diagrams of how to fall on your knees and tremble
while in this fly speck on the vast waters
rub the heart raw and its journey
hoist your bones above your skin
but right now I'm strangely calm
even with my fear of drowning

out there I can see a lit porthole
no ship   just a window afloat above the swell
through it there's a large room

where the dancing was done
couples held each other and no one was clumsy
there was no fear till the caresses began
the faintings of miracles that crisscross the body
the sighings of the unplaceable
that take reality away in an instant
the ballroom gone below and all music lost

how calm I feel at this moment
even if the wrathful deities that resemble dark coats adrift
were to appear suddenly and absolutely
with finish lines for talons   lifelines for ribs
I wouldn't be afraid   not now.

THE PARTICULARS OF POINTED THINGS

lifetime after lifetime they met
always like two voices over a stranger's body
over someone sleeping under heavy blankets
someone you mustn't wake

they were on this journey
and with each life a weight was added
and a weight was taken away

so it was always the beginning
so it always took time for them to recognize each other

without chance pushing its pins into reality
without the particulars of pointed things

but chance rose each time
the fulfilment of time
like fingers on piano keys
fulfil music yet to be born

they had known each other from the beginning
when there was only one day for every two evenings
when the only begettings were rocks falling to earth
when love was already venerable   a matter of clairvoyance
a bodiless breathing that came close
to what the heart would be.

THE GRASS WIDOW

there was a wind moving through the trees
trees the colour of hands held firmly in the dark

it was autumn so the shadows had daughters
to arrange the places for shadows to lie
sons to go to Egypt and return with a blackness
to fill the house by the river
the house of the elderly asleep beside the river

no pain in September except from that house
for miles around only woods where the clouds
spread to a single form   the cloud-shape
of the moon in her boat and leaves upon the water

the wind found the house and stood for a moment
in the wood of the house   in the nails driven beyond light
Spanish nails still bright as constellations in the beams

and found one woman lying there
one old woman among many
lying and dropping words into sleep
one with hands folded
with cheekbones like hairpins
holding up tightly the lower half of her face

and the wind thought that was beauty
that soft body   that hush of cells
those weights and measures
where the soul honed its skills
at waking up among fabulous creatures
that walked the pavements

made bread   drove trucks
carried children on their backs

and the wind blew a strand of hair across her face
because that was touching her
that was being there
the shadows being there and the trees
because that gesture was eternity
and eternity was all the wind could
ever hold in its arms.

THE SAYINGS OF DARK SPACE UPON THE BODY

for Jeannette and Munro

tonight beneath a moon of black rope   a moon coiled invisible
beneath stars made of music and fire   Mozart and matches
you light the lamp and open the curtains as if you were
parting paper clouds on stage at Monsieur Follain's Theatre
you sit in your chair with a theatrical longing
for angels as thin as canaries
wanting all of silent paradise in their seats
the picture palace tilting into view
spreading lights on the lights you made on earth
the years you spent illuminating
words you spoke to no one in particular
the sleep of sleep on tongue and page

out your window the tub of heaven rusts with light
the trees rust with peace
beyond those hills armies and priests lie in their tenements
singing each other to sleep
recounting their campaigns against their master
that abstraction both ancestral and bright
as words they never speak
a wilderness of things said between pillow and rain
between the breath on the sheet and the breath on the sea

a breeze blows the scarves of the flea
and the cowlicks of every cat
who hears thunder in the growing
of each grass blade on the hill
and what arrives comes by way of a carnelian
by the colour of a carnelian

colour of beeswax in the stomach of a bear
colour of poor treasures hidden for too long in the earth
which is the starlight hanging like belting over the horizon
guiding each hungry sleeper to its table of words
a locution of appearance
the sayings of dark space upon the body
the body's surcoat like a sense of language lost
among addictions to pale floors and lacquered clocks

by way of a star   by the colour of a star
a planet stands against a wall turning
saying good night and good night
this is or may be a greeting and not a farewell
not the hush of a sad world with its arms at its sides
not the sad weight of those arms upon the soil
but a globe content with all these secret meetings
between wind and stone and flesh
the gossip that breaks the rock   that kills the innocent
that kills the chaos of a given day
because time and death are gossip only
none of it as true as your eyes
filling space with countless stars
that swarm of fires being a self
you breathe against in the dark

a saviour   an emptiness   the hand you hold.

ARROWS

the secret places have surfaces
    good for dancing
a young girl and her mother dance there
    together they make a wisdom
you could carry in your pocket to the office
    a remembrance you could feel
through all the fox hunts of the computers

there are rumours that move through the office air like
the Lord of Silence through the endless
pieces of paper and fallen hair

in times of pain red flowers grow on the
office walls like hellish roses
their long stems cross-threaded with salt and flesh

the secret places are great quiet laps
you can dance upon   where you can hide
all the things you steal and deserve
all the goodselves dipped in mystery

the secret places are like bowstrings pulled taut

arrows fly through the office
there are hauntings upon the arrows
there are whispers upon the arrows

then the music of a mother and a little girl spinning
which is the swish of arrows through the air
which is the sigh when you are hit deeply
when time lowers its flag and you hear small hours

cranes bending wing-beats in their eggs
mice waking in the wolf's belly
the stragglers
the salmon exacting presence
which means worlds multiplied upon worlds
arrows sung through flesh
a joy unmixed and uncared for shifting
through the office light
stragglers seated at their desks   the adored.

IV

CHILD OF THE EARTH

TWELVE CORNERS OF THE EARTH

JANUARY

flensed snow packed under birches
array of fox tracks hosting divinity and its absence
monstrance as eternal hunger with a fox's breath
murmuring a superstition of wounds
onto everything that moves

snow records the passing of each reach across its surface
the running fox   the dreaming man
withdrawn stubbornly into hours
history was made for snow   it gives it something to do
takes on each second and its interlacings
unlearnt it unlearns and so knows the terrain well
that place where we walk to lose our way
years remembered as minutes
departures bent   arrivals churned up
all footprints removing themselves from a wintry ground.

FEBRUARY

blizzard and one consciousness of the blizzard
turns an overspill of firs near the cliff edge
to hear the downbeat of the ocean under its ice
ice is a scriptorium whether over water or in the air
the written word gone mad and contained

shoulder blades of the storm push birds to earth
making other entry points to Aeon
so that a frozen gull on the beach
is the sentient fall through time
ecstasy of lost settlements   the planet turning.

MARCH

each star retires   each claw goes out like a flame
shadowed morning across the hard snow
a voice slips its teeth between the branches
but doesn't bite down on anything
coyote frieze just there where the light
softens against the trail
where the inner path leads
to what's unfinished beneath the skin

every spruce lives in itself
reigns nowhere and so proceeds to cover ground
with needles pointing to all that's unborn
roots made to follow every living thing home to its bed
silent and indriven towards the last remembered sleep.

APRIL

snow melts along earshot
mice quiet as doorjambs   spider eggs piping
just a little under stones
grass two wing-beats away from light
all the dead sparrows returning to their nests

the road went back there
where trees roost upon the emptiness
to find shadows of untraceable labours
interwoven with black ferns and twigs
oleograph of seeming
still life rippled by a transcendence on its rounds
the blind corners of rainy days
thunder's pull on rabbit fur
and a ditch of fire thrown to earth.

MAY

deeper than the eloquence of a stone's tremolo
buds like lambs bleating among the corbels
of clouds and blood's inventions
cries hunkered in a leaf rise out of the skin
as words describing the unknowable

an overspread of glassy light among the rookeries
eggs blanching mystery with feathers pale and unborn
nests tightened to voices soaring out of nothingness
sagging of birth over raindrops and granite
there are still cold nights that require these fires
all the undecipherable burnings of accession
the first good blush that warms the world.

JUNE

these last hours have been stacked atop heads
wet with ditch water   toes starched with sleep
tongues soft with a mizzling of this green hill
the eye's tent billows from dreams
nurseries infallible   litters as certain
as fingers round a stone

so early risers unclasp the margins
to join the day's centre
bats trawl the air one last time
feeling sunlight   trees come climbing out of the earth
and a morning breeze stirs the intelligence of leaves
their numbering of themselves
which is a counting of every possible thing.

JULY

daylight is the sun's alibi
heat deepening in the long grass
reason enough for it to transfer along desire
any possibility   any longing   frenzy
with that final clench before death is made

the sun's ores and storms continually melt
fold   unfold   drift into a bear's fur
a bear crossing a dusty riverbed
dreaming of catching an endless fish
lifting the latch of a hive
opening the berry's dark arms.

AUGUST

at night stars are hearts echoing back to bone
by morning clouds walk on water
by noon eagles tremble at their oars
at dusk the whole slump of the planet to its ion
pinches of clotting and ectoplasm
leakage of orbiting spooks
in the shabby glade

summer hunched in the weedy furrows
can't sleep for this one moment
the turning of the year   the crisp leaf
its grave goods merely voices on the forest floor
ants listen to those chemicals   jaws that ripen inward
rotting of edges spoken across damp ground
the decay of things once said with the heart rate of suns.

SEPTEMBER

blinds are closed quietly between the trees
which makes the stars rise   moon cross the sky
oil lamps drift between the planets

all month vanishing points begin hiding the hawk's talons
the wolf's teeth   human hands
rivers carry threads of glamour to the backwaters
minerals lie unconsoled among the root hairs of maples
finding their way back to blood and form
is finding their way through the dark of several worlds
where our desires do not appear.

OCTOBER

wrong moments gone cold in the sunlight
leaf scars lingering in the upper air
microscopic foundlings and cutthroats
almost apologetic under the dry leaves
now that summer is over
and blood looks so precious against the moss

vagaries collected with a turn of the wind
mythy deaths finally realized   finally spoken of
among the tribes of soil and water
braced like great nations for the horizon
that comes at last to carry their children to belief.

NOVEMBER

limbo of autumn grass and the carpentry of trees
misting of blood across stone
hunters return while the sky's munitions explode
in silence above their rifles
return with pre-Copernican dogs
who view the world as centred revelation

moonlight fortified by pilgrims lost and pilgrims yet to be
eventually guides the deer across freckled ground
with eyes like pistils burning
ears shawled in sounds that knowing makes
settling into death
that stalk of breath that fills the spine
with Paradise and leads us all away.

DECEMBER

training for snow the hills cover themselves in memory
knee-deep it haunts the bracken as algae does the shore
the spirit shifted is the movement of Mnemosyne
verge of her who taught the rose hips to behold

and at night the smell of bedrooms between the alders
sleep lost to final fadings of dependable asylums
storms shied away hold their place and processions
wait till remembering dies past knowing
till the future is constant   eating the light
cells dying   believing in lotions and balms
the antidote to frosted bone   pill in the moonlight.

GENESIS

I'm walking through a slow shower
the scarification of the earth holds me up
birds fly low over the ground
far off through the trees a low thunder
still further rooms with people
listening to radios   removing books from shelves
holding each other with clasped hands

the day is warm like a miracle known
by only one person for a long time
the hour's blueprint is unfolded
everyone looks for entrances and exits
placing an x where they might be standing
then rushing carelessly into walls

I'm trying to make my way back to the car
but find the ocean instead
adjusting its body to suit the sand grains
that separate it from empty space

I sit on a grey boulder to watch the waves
then the downpour suddenly arrives
bringing together the corners of existence
so you feel no reason to move an inch

what happened forever is happening now
I can't stand even if I wanted to
because silence searches my body to find her children
because this is the way the world is born.

BANNS

these birds are all the wedding dresses of the world
these trees all the brides waiting

you can begin no journey here without marriage

when I arrived I knew the shadow
would be long and hard to follow
shadow of a matchmaker stretching thinly through the grass
but I came to walk here
to marry the heartbeats that collect
on birch leaves after rain has fallen
the minute ones without home or chest in which to beat
without blood to send pouring through the silence

I love what can't be seen   I marry what can't be seen
and so walk through the forest via homages
the invisible knowing of no hand that it hasn't held
no hand without a wedding ring like a quiet storm
moving round a finger
shy gold that carries every moment darkened on currents
studies of one flesh
every bird in the air.

CHILD OF THE EARTH

1

at evening the musk of falling snow reaches the earth
snow that will fall all night   turning round in pivots of space
spaces centred on moonlight   the moonlit ridges
of the self that abounds

so many selves make up the nightly routines   so many
fall with the snow upon the land   drown in the wintry sea

the body sits and the snow drifts down at light's end
the self drifts into woods and hills
arriving long after the world was made
the dark somewheres already in place and folded
as if time had passed   folded as you suppose it would be
if you arrived late to sit alone among the trees
among the cool embraces   the awayness of snow.

2

sitting in the woods you think of other worlds
planets where snow also falls   sulphur snows   iodine snows
the arsenic snows of Saturn   neptunium snows
toothed hills filling with empurpled flakes of neon
this great depth of distances is comforting
among pine trees who have no inheritors but themselves
beside the river frozen to a strength
that would break if it moved
and you think of things that you can't bear without shadows
leaning in upon your flesh   all the semblances leaning there.

3

snow heals the moment's burn
which is bright as Alpha Cygnus
of fixed position   of infinite birth
of indissoluble address
heals the wound that secretes its appetite upon you
knives that shave solace below the flesh

you sit as snow drops past the meridian
past the cuffs of trees
down among the inscrutable levels
to atoms forgetting reality
to a bare place where all visible things appear
as shades if they appear at all
ghosting around the emptiness
calling the elements home to their beds
home to every harm left unattended
a winter that surrounds you   seeable among the trees.

4

for many lifetimes the snow fell and you were the stillness
positioned there
you were the mechanics of snow and twisted ends of stars
structures of the self growing and fading into birth

O child of the earth you are me and us and the rabbit
who has believed longer than we have   purling evocations
in his warren like blood moving through its tunnels
seeking the backs of our legs   the palms of our hands
the movement it feasts upon   the edible motion

you're the pond pushing life out from its centre
cord grass drunk along the shore   bees pouring out of amber
all this which is part of the self   the cool of the night
the fire behind us we rarely see   quietude
you're the ocean setting forth   the first stone it touches
the wind that will blow the snow away
blow your particles into empty space   O empty space
this is the self   all worlds   the single place.

NOTE ON THE TEXT

Some of these poems first appeared in *Canadian Author*, *Pottersfield Portfolio*, and *Undertow*.

*

The author is grateful to the Canada Council for its financial assistance.